Edward Dafydd Morris

Inaugural Discourses of Professors Morris and Nelson

Delivered at Lane Theological Seminary, on the thirty-second anniversary

May 13-14, 1868. Together with a brief sketch of the Institution and the

annual report of the Treasurer, F. V. Chamberlai

Edward Dafydd Morris

Inaugural Discourses of Professors Morris and Nelson
*Delivered at Lane Theological Seminary, on the thirty-second anniversary May
13-14, 1868. Together with a brief sketch of the Institution and the annual report of
the Treasurer, F. V. Chamberlai*

ISBN/EAN: 9783337097035

Printed in Europe, USA, Canada, Australia, Japan

Cover: Foto ©Lupo / pixelio.de

More available books at **www.hansebooks.com**

Inaugural Discourses,

OF

Professors Morris and Nelson,

DELIVERED AT

Lane Theological Seminary,

ON THE

THIRTY-SECOND ANNIVERSARY

May 13–14, 1868.

Together with a brief Sketch of the Institution,
and the Annual Report of the Treasurer,
F. V. Chamberlain.

———•———

CINCINNATI:
PUBLISHED BY THE BOARD OF TRUSTEES.
1868.
ELM STREET PRINTING COMPANY.

THE inauguration of REV. EDWARD D. MORRIS, as Professor of *Ecclesiastical History and Church Polity*, and REV. HENRY A. NELSON as Professor of *Systematic and Pastoral Theology*, took place in the afternoon of Wednesday, May 13; the services being conducted by REV. G. M. MAXWELL, D. D., President of the Board of Trust. After the reading of appropriate passages of Scripture and prayer by REV. DANIEL RICE, D. D., the Professors elect were formally inducted into office, and were earnestly and solemnly charged by the President, to be faithful to the sacred trust now committed to them. This ceremony was followed by the inaugural discourse of Professor MORRIS, on *The Supernatural Quality of the Church of God.* The discourse of Professor NELSON, on *The Relations of Christian Truth to Christian Life*, was delivered on the following day, at the close of the anniversary exercises.

DISCOURSE.

THE SUPERNATURAL QUALITY OF THE CHURCH OF GOD.

THE speculative unbelief of the seventeenth century, incarnated in the person of Thomas Hobbes, declared the church to be simply an arbitrary contrivance of human society:—an organization devised by men for the purpose of securing the more readily certain social and political ends, and having neither existence nor authority except by the *imprimatur* of the State. The more philosophic skepticism of the nineteenth century recognizes that church as something more than a political device—a tributary institution adhering to the civil power, as the mistletoe clings to the oak: yet attributes its origin exclusively to the moral instincts of mankind, and denies to it any validity or authority, beyond what it may possess as the product of our spiritual nature. Both agree in rejecting the cardinal truth, that *this church is a divine institution :* springing neither from civil enactment nor from moral instinct, but originating in the mind of God, and by Him implanted in the earth for purposes higher far than any which either political necessi-

ties or spiritual impulses would inspire man to seek.
A philosophy more broad and just combines with
the Holy Scripture to affirm that this remarkable
institution is not to be viewed as, in any essential
sense, the contrivance or creation of man: but
rather as the manifest product of the same benefi-
cent Being who framed the worlds by His power,
and who in infinite love gave to mankind the gospel
of His dear Son. Precious truth: questioned indeed by that skepticism which would reduce all
things to the low level of sight and of nature, yet
as worthy of universal acceptance as the fact of
creation, or the doctrine of redemption in Christ
Jesus!

But this is only a portion of the truth. The
church is not merely superhuman in its origin: it is
supernatural in essence, in vitality, in development.
Implanted in the earth by the hand of God, it has
not been left to unfold and bloom there under the
action of natural or visible agencies simply: taking
its place, like the family, in the great plan of Providence, and under that plan rising like a tribe or an
empire to its present eminence. In no improper
sense of the term, the church of God on earth is
a continuous and germinant miracle: living from
age to age only because He abides in it perpetu-
ally: increasing in luxuriance and fruitfulness, century on century, only because He pours into it
his own perennial life. Standing in the plan of
grace, rather than the plan of Providence, her
superhuman origin becomes the preface to an equally
superhuman existence and unfolding. As John be-
held her in apocalyptic vision, descending from
heaven, and adorned with the complete perfections

of the millennial state, so she descended from heaven at the first: and her entire career has been that of a celestial visitant, inspired continually by divine impulses, and continually led by a divine hand, in her gracious ministry to the soul of man. Her life is the life of God: her existence and her course constantly attest His presence and His power. More precious truth: unseen by the dim eye of a perverted nature, and rejected by a philosophy as pretentious as it is skeptical, yet obvious to all who study the history of that church with unperverted vision, and above all price in the esteem of those who dwell within her shelter, and are conscious of her nurturing and hallowing power!

In this wiser and purer spirit, let us meditate together upon the theme thus presented for our consideration: THE SUPERNATURAL QUALITY OF THE CHURCH OF GOD. To such consideration we are summoned by far higher incentives than any that may be derived from the peculiar solemnities of this occasion, or from the contemplation of those specific and difficult duties with which I have just been officially intrusted. The skeptical assaults upon the career and doctrine, and even the validity and authority of the church; the papal and prelatic tendency toward the humanization of the church at the sacrifice of her spiritual supremacy; the yearnings and efforts toward closer fellowship among those who are conscious of belonging to her holy and catholic communion, alike demand that we should possess the clearest, soundest views of that central and divine quality in the church, whose presence manifested puts both unbelief and priestly assumption to silence, gives rest to controversy,

calms division, and unites all who are consciously
the children of God in one common and blessed
household of faith. Let us, therefore, as disciples
of Christ rather than students of history, first contemplate *the great fact* thus suggested, and then
consider in brief certain *practical bearings of this
fact* upon our belief and our duty.

I. One prominent illustration of this supernatural quality may be found in the sphere of *doctrine :*
that inspired series or system of truths, which constitute the intellectual basis of this divine institution. It is an obvious and significant fact, that such
a foundation of doctrine is a peculiar feature of the
church of God.   Heathenism, whether modern or
ancient, blossoms into temples and altars and gorgeous rites; under the influence of classic or ori-
ental philosophy, it sometimes takes on the aspect
of profound speculation; but never does it ripen
into doctrine. Like other human efforts in the region of the ideal, it only reflects, even when it
wears the appearance of truth, the degenerate tem-
per of the source whence it sprang. Not even the
elaborate Deism of the eighteenth century, surrep-
titiously appropriating from the Christian system
such cardinal features as the existence and providence of God, and the immortality of man, and the
immutability and worth of virtue ; or even the Positive Religion of our day, professing to despise and
demolish Christianity, yet building its grand temple of devotion with material clandestinely taken
from the ruins, will furnish an exception to this
universal law. Man by nature is competent to fab-
ricate philosophies, or invent forms of worship; but

he is not competent to fashion for himself a system
of doctrine. Erring on one side, through narrow-
ness of vision, and on the other through dimness of
appreciation, failing here to comprehend, and there
to include, baffled continually by prejudice, by self-
love, by natural hostility to truth, as well as by defective power to discern it, his best attempts in
this direction will be but speculations unable to
command his own respect, and utterly devoid of
power to control the assent, or win the loyal and
trustful love of others.

It is in the church of God alone, that such a system of doctrine is found:—a system embracing
within its scope the grandest themes, presenting
these with utmost fullness and clearness, and in
such methods as to secure for them the reverence
of our intellect, and the strongest affections of the
heart. There is no truth which it is important for
man, as a spiritual being, to know during the present life, concerning which that system does not
speak in clear, faithful, persuasive terms. The nature, and character, and ways of God, His adminis-
tration of providence, and of grace, and His plan
of mercy for a lost world; the character, and need,
and duty of man; the methods and the vast possi-
bilities of redemption; the present life with its
spheres, offices, responsibilities, and the life to come,
full of glory for the sanctified, and of wrath for the
sinner; these all are set forth in the Bible more
comprehensively, more clearly, more urgently than
in all other books combined. And so exact, simple,
philosophic is the method of this Revelation—so
thoughtful and tender is the spirit breathing
through the whole—so full of blending authority

and grace, and so inspiring in the sweet hopes it
justifies, that it spontaneously wins for itself a purer
assent, a more complete acceptance, than any which
human philosophy ever gained—any which the
most splendid heathenism ever inspired.

Whence came this wonderful system of doctrine,
the recognized basis of the church of God on earth?
Is it some unique product of human genius, standing forever like the Parthenon or the Paradise Lost,
unrivaled and unapproachable? Is it the last and
highest exhibition of the speculative insight of the
race—the *ultima thule* of human research in the
sphere of religion? Is it not rather from God—a
revelation directly from the skies? Such is the
amazing, yet unquestionable fact. The truths of
religion are supernatural truths—supernatural in
their essence and their grouping—supernatural in
the modes wherein they are presented, and in their
influence and effect. They are such truths as we
could never have adequately discerned; their com-
bination is such as we could never have contrived.
They have a celestial fragrance upon them—they
glow and glisten as if God himself were shining
through them. Surely this revelation came not in old
time by the will of man: surely holy men of God
spake herein, as they were moved by the Holy Ghost.
Be our theory of inspiration what it may, we must
recognize in this system a divine quality and sig-
nificance—the signature of God Himself in the
handwriting of mortals. And as it was thus supernatural in its first manifestation, so a wisdom more
than human has controlled its subsequent unfold-
ings. The entire progress of doctrine, both during
the New Testament era, and through the succeed-

ing centuries, illustrates the same divine presence and supervision. Though the Holy Spirit ceased His work of inspiration with the Revelation of Saint John, fitly making His final visit to that one who was the heavenliest, as he was the last in the apostolic circle; yet, who can doubt that it was He who afterward raised up men like Athanasius and Augustine, Luther and Calvin, to be expositors of the truth thus communicated—or that it was His hand that brought the church to those great crises in her doctrinal career, wherein the cardinal features of the gospel system successively received their formal definition, and become fixed and imperishable elements in our holy faith?

Nor is this view invalidated by the fact that both in the original inspiring, and in the subsequent unfolding of this system of doctrine, human and even sinful instrumentalities have been blended with this divine agency. It is indeed an obvious fact, that the supernatural light beaming upon us in the Scripture, is in every case colored and refracted to some degree by the earthly media through which it shines; prophets and apostles not only speaking in their native words, but also employing molds and forms of thought suitable to their own nature; so that, while we everywhere behold divinity glowing and flashing forth with an unquestioned effulgence, we also everywhere discern the man standing in his separate personality, and imparting his own peculiarities to what he is commissioned to reveal. It is no less obvious that, in the case of those who receive and interpret this Revelation, we may detect the same molding or determining influence exerted by personal condition and culture and char.

acter, each grasping and appropriating the verities of grace in methods and degrees peculiar to himself—or that the belief of the church in general has thus been colored, modified, limited, and even distorted and corrupted, by the same human influences. It is in this way only that we can account for those imperfections, those variations, those collisions in the sphere of doctrine, which are so apparent in the record of church history; or for those errors and heresies—those defective or perverse presentations of the truth, which stain these records on every page. The natural, with its limitations and its defects, has continually mingled with the supernatural, and has left the traces of its marring fingers on every sacred article and tenet of the gospel scheme. But how wonderfully has that supernatural element retained its supremacy, and how manifestly does the vital doctrine of the church demonstrate a divine origin, a divine unfolding, a divine presence and supervision at every stage!

II. A second illustration of this supernatural quality may be obtained in the department of *experience*—that experience which is everywhere recognized as the spiritual and essential life, just as her doctrine is the recognized intellectual foundation of the church of God. If the truths of Scripture, like those of science or of philosophy, related only to the analysis and grouping of fact, the exposition of natural laws, or the fashioning of ideal abstractions, their influence upon the religious living of mankind would be but indirect and inconsiderable. Boastful as their votaries generally are, the effects of these agencies upon the moral sentiment and demeanor of the world, are very gradual at the best, and often hardly distinguishable. The great currents of conduct and of character, whether individual or organic, flow on notwithstanding such scientific or philosophic impediments, essentially unmodified, essentially unimproved. Sin rules and reigns with little perceptible variation, whether under the teaching of the Baconian system, or in countries where the name of the sage of Verulam was never spoken. Sin rules and reigns in scientific France, as in barbaric Abyssinia, varied indeed in form and in degree of grossness, yet developed into even greater and darker maturity. The classification of facts into the forms of elaborate science does not arrest it. The announcement of laws, sublime as those of Kepler or Newton, hardly effects it. Whether the ideal or the realistic methods of speculation be in the ascendant, it still rules and reigns, and humanity is still its victim. And were our race subjected to no reformatory influence beyond that which science and philosophy are supplying—were the regeneration of mankind dependent solely on these corrective agencies, elevating and inspiring though they be, there is every reason for believing that human character would continue to be substantially what it now is—that the experience of the world would be an experience of sin forever.

But the doctrines of the church of God are not of this type. They indeed present facts, suggest classifications, disclose laws, embody a profound and a divine philosophy. But the facts are facts concerning ourselves as moral beings—the classifications are based on diversities in character—the laws are laws for our spiritual guidance—the phi-

losophy is concentrated around to the two foci of sin
and redemption. The golden truths of Scripture
possess this rare eminence: that they are directly
transmutable into character. As the intellect per-
ceives them, the heart is affected by them: as they
enter and inspire the heart, they gather around them
its best affections—they become the germinating
force of its purest impulses and its grandest motives.
Accepted by the soul, they immediately penetrate
and vitalize it. They arrest its previous inclinations,
turn its purposes into new channels, suffuse it with
fresh energy, change and elevate its whole life. Especially when these doctrines are set forth in the
immaculate personality of Christ—uttered in His
words, illustrated in His example, confirmed in His
atoning death, do they thus become the vital seeds
of a new experience, reaching powers and sensibilities which the most profound science never
could approach—penetrating the moral nature with
a force utterly unfamiliar to philosophy, and affecting changes therein, which are worthy to be
called a new creation. His teachings and example
and spirit, and especially His superhuman personality, present these in forms which spontaneously awaken the interest alike of sage and of
savage, and which may become the germs of a new
manhood in the grossest barbarian of Central Africa
as in the gravest philosopher of Central Europe.
There is something divine in these doctrines, as incarnated in the Messiah, which all men are as quick
to feel and reverence as to perceive—a supernatural
clearness, pertinence, grandeur, solemnity, which
suggest the very presence of Deity in them, and
which invest them with a spiritual potency infin-
itely beyond that of all truth beside.

But the celestial origin of these doctrines, their peculiar reflection of the divine personality, their manifest supernaturalness in substance and in adaptation, will not alone account for their amazing influence on the life of the church. The same Book which reveals them, declares that in their august entrance into the soul of man, and in their signal operations upon the character, they are supernaturally endorsed, vitalized, rendered impressive and effectual. It declares on the other hand, that the vision of man is supernaturally prepared to perceive them—that the religious susceptibilities are divinely awakened to embrace them, and that the will and choice are directly moved by the Spirit of God to receive and obey them. Mysterious fact—more strange than any manifestation of that mystic *vis naturæ* which both quickens the buried grain, and prepares the cold earth to welcome and nurture it —more wondrous than that fascinating potency of true eloquence, which sways and moves a listening multitude, as the ripening grain is swayed by a sweeping wind. Mysterious fact, essentially supernatural in quality, and beyond the reach of visible demonstration, yet rendered palpable and sure by results which can be explained in no other way, and whose vast magnitude sufficiently attests the potency as well as reality of the agent that produced them. The truth of God thus has its counterpart and complement in the Spirit of God, and the operations of that Spirit in the experience and life of the church, like the influence of that truth upon her understanding and faith, certify abundantly to her divine quality, and her consequent claim on human interest and respect.

For, the type of experience thus induced, is as peculiar as the source from which it springs. The true manhood in Christ, shaped by His love, animated by His spirit, conformed progressively to His example, maturing into some measure of His perfection, is as really miraculous as was the raising of Lazarus from the dead—a greater miracle, both because it is a resurrection of the dead soul to newness of life, and also, because it involves the exhibition of higher qualities, the exercise of more tender and precious grace, in Him who performs it. From that manhood, how much of the common experience of mankind is excluded—the sins, the indulgences, the neglect of right, the wrong tastes and tendencies of the world! How much is included in it, of which that world knows nothing—the sweet graces that bloom in it like roses in a garden, the pure virtues that adorn it like statues in a palace, the bright hopes and aspirations that deck it as sunset decks and glorifies the sky! And when we come to realize that this type of manhood is not attained in some rare instance, under some signal and unparalleled culture of grace, but is reproduced in myriads of cases, as if the Immanuel had raised the dead whithersoever he went through Judea and Galilee—that this newness of life has been manifested through the Spirit in different lands and ages, among peoples the most various, in circumstances most diverse, as in instances beyond computation—that this moral experience in all these instances has been essentially the same, not simply from the days of Christ down to our times, but even during the period of prophet and psalmist and judge, and in the primitive age of patriarchs, when

Enoch walked with God exactly as the Christian now walks with Jesus—and that all these, made one by the sharing of this one spiritual life, are divinely joined together in the one holy and catholic church, existing through all ages, and including all the elect from the beginning to the end of time —when we come to realize this, shall we not pronounce that church supernatural in experience as in doctrine, and reverently rejoice in it as the ordained household of God upon earth!

III. A third illustration of the supernatural quality under consideration, may be derived from the *organization* and the *growth* of this earthly church. What has already been said, justifies the anticipation that those in whom such a belief and such a life are found, will not only be separated by wide lines of demarcation from the remainder of mankind, but will also in virtue of these common traits, be joined together in a fellowship as peculiar, permanent, precious as the spiritual foundations whereon it reposes. For such fellowship God has made external provisions: adjusting the social nature and habits of man to its higher necessities, organizing the family and the state to be its antetypes, arranging the whole order of the world with reference to its development. The church thus stands as a central and a controlling feature in the divine plan of things—like a palace located in the center of some splendid landscape, wherein every tree and shrub and flower are manifestly so arranged as to enhance the beauty, comfort and attractiveness of the central structure. But this external provision, impressive as it becomes when properly studied, has its key or explanation only in the social and asso-

ciative character of all genuine piety—in the vital
brotherhood of all who receive the doctrine and
possess the life of God in Christ. The church lies
constructively in the sanctified nature of believers,
as the fruit lies imbosomed in the fragrant, rosy
blossom. They who by faith are constituted the
true sons of God, are therefore brethren: and every
instinct of their sanctified being impels them to
give expression to this sense of fraternity in sweet
communion, in mutual prayer and praise, in all
practical forms of spiritual fellowship. Wherever
two or three of these are met together in the
uniting mood of piety, there the church as well as
the Savior is present—there are the beginnings of
a genuine household of God. In this internal community of belief and of experience, we discern the
correlative explanation of the external plan: the
providence apparent in the latter, changing insensi-
bly into the wondrous grace that produces and
inspires the former.

How far, therefore, below the blessed truth, are
the skeptical suggestions that the church is an ar-
tificial contrivance of state-craft, or a spontaneous
product of unsanctified human sensibilities! We
behold in her an institution as truly incorporated
into the Divine plan of things for our world as is
the family or the state: and in the spiritual material provided for her in souls sanctified through the
indwelling truth and life of God, we discern still
more conclusive evidence that she has indeed descended from Him out of heaven. Upon every one
who claims a place within that sacred enclosure
without the antecedent attainment of a Christian
manhood, though sprinkled with priestly hyssop or

even robed with priestly investiture, how fearfully does He hurl His solemn anathema! And how like a storm at midnight on the tossing ocean, ablaze with lightnings, echoing with thunders, is His awful *maranatha* pronounced upon those organizations bearing the name, imitating the forms, assuming the prerogatives of His church, yet devoid of faith, of life, of spiritual power! Such counterfeits only prove the worth of the sacred reality which they seek to imitate; and the poor and frail humanity they betray, only brings into view by touching contrast the superhuman excellence inhering in the reality itself.

These statements respecting the church as a Divine organization receive ample confirmation in the various methods or processes wherein that organization has been historically brought toward maturity. We first observe this church revealing its existence within the circle of the household; dwelling in tents with the patriarchs, as the angels once tarried with Abraham, and there through simplest rites and offerings nurturing the faith of ancient saints. We then observe it gradually passing into the tribal and the national form, both broadening its sphere and enlarging its functions; and at length under Moses assuming its appropriate theocratic type, and becoming coterminous with the Hebrew state. Thus enfolded in the nation, as the living kernel is enfolded in the rough husk, it passed ere long into the age of psalm and of prophecy, when the voice of symbolic ceremony began to be lost in the clearer voice of inspired intimation, foretelling and heralding the Messianic dawn. At length under Christ and his apostles, we observe it taking worthier shape at Jerusa-

2

lem, at Antioch, at Corinth and elsewhere, preserving whatever was precious in the Jewish synagogue
or temple, borrowing something from the forms of
civil power, yet retaining through all these changes
its spiritual identity and its essential life. After the
apostolic period we observe it slowly passing under
the shadow of human pride and ambition, surrender-
ing to centralizing tendencies and prelatic assump-
tions, and in the degenerate process losing both
spirituality and power;—then entering the deadly
eclipse of the Papacy, when men like the Gregories
and the Innocents wore the tiara of spiritual, and
even of temporal dominion in its name—when its
doctrines were subordinated to the traditions of men
and its sacred rites were perverted into showy and
fruitless forms, and its pure life struggled faintly
forth beneath the mass of human corruption, as some
pure spring on the mountain side trickles feebly
through a dense land-slide that has come down upon
it. From this era of declension, but not of death,
we observe it in the Reformation rising again into
both a higher form and a nobler experience, returning for its lost polity neither to councils nor fathers but to the Holy Word, yet interpreting this
in conformity with the spirit and usages of modern life;
and in a free Protestantism, both incorporating the
best elements of the past, and preparing the way for a
larger, nobler future. And in these transitions from
the patriarchal to the theocratic and prophetic form,
and from the rudimental church of apostolic times
to the matured organizations now extant; compact,
yet not centralized, strong yet not tyrannical, honor-
ing the divine doctrine as the only law of faith,
preserving the divine life as the only bond of fel-

lowship, and even amid many diversities illustrating the real oneness, the spiritual glory of the true Household of Faith, who does not discern not merely an enduring vitality, but also a palpable progress, a progressive advance toward perfection, such as could have been devised and executed by Deity alone!

In whatever aspect we contemplate the actual history of that church, we are brought to the same result. Look at its continuous existence. It reaches backward to the plains of Haran, to the summits of Ararat, to the sacred scenes wherein holy men walked with God in the morning of the world. It was more fully organized under Abraham and his descendants, before Rome was, or Greece had assumed her place in history. It grew and matured while Babylon was rising into eminence: it was extant when Alexander reigned and the Cæsars stamped all countries with the Roman name. It lived and bloomed while all else of ancient civilization was dying: it survived the long winter of the dark ages, like a plant bedded in the soil below the range of frost or of storm. It rose again in the bright springtime of the Reformation: it put forth bud and blossom in the centuries following: and still it lives and blooms with a vigor, an amplitude, a luxuriant fruitfulness unknown in any preceding age. Look at its remarkable diffusion, from that central cradle of the race where its existence began, and from that narrow strip of land on the Mediterranean where it first assumed the national form, into Western Asia, into the main seats of power and of learning in Southern Europe, among the nations and races dwelling on the Rhine, the Seine, the Thames: crossing oceans and conquering new continents, returning to traverse the plains of the Orient and the wilds of Africa, at home everywhere and triumphant everywhere, until it has become almost as extensive as the world. Look at its manifest progress, not alone in doctrine, and experience, and polity, but also in numbers and allies, in tributary resources, in external position and influence, in alliances with art and culture and the finest civilization—in a word, in all those earthly elements that seem to insure to it a perpetuity of prominence in the earth. Surely we can explain such phenomena, and such a development, only on the plain hypothesis that this church in history as in origin is of God.

It is true, that this growth, so palpably supernatural, has been continually repressed, diverted, stayed by the malevolent action of human sin. How often have heresies, not always morbific, but rather the inflammatory stages introductory to a more healthful life, yet always fraught with danger and stimulative of unhallowed passion, excited and disturbed the church! How often has a corrupting formalism perverted the rites of the church into mystical and powerless forms, changed her doctrines into the shibboleths of a sect, polluted the fountains of her spiritual life! How frequently has human ambition, often under the garb of the priesthood, crept into the church, not in the sphere of polity alone, but also along multiplied other avenues, administering this divine trust for personal advantage, or in the aggrandizing interest of party? How frequently has that spirit of worldliness which once filled the Jewish temple with the changers of money, in other times profaned the hallowed courts of the church, and made them a house of merchandise! All the forces and capabilities of the sinful heart, all the influences of natural and degenerate society, as well as all the powers and principalities of darkness, have thus been arrayed against the progress of this church of God. Seductive fashions have vainly sought to beguile it; political instrumentalities have been invoked in vain to overthrow it; the Goliaths of unbelief have stood up against it, and have fallen; the arts of man and the wiles of the devil have been unable to subvert it. And how shall we account for a history like this, in the midst of such deadly antagonisms, if we do not assume that this is indeed a supernatural church; supernatural in doctrine and experience, and no less supernatural in organization and in growth!

1. Accepting now the precious fact thus in part illustrated, we may briefly notice some of the bearings of this fact upon our belief and our duty, observing first, *the peculiar confirmation herein afforded to the entire Christian system.* It is a most remarkable provision of divine grace, which anticipates the developing perplexities of faith and the augmenting skepticism of the world, by arranging a progressive series of witnesses to the truth, whose testimony should become intelligible only through the lapse of time, and whose full and convincing witness should be summoned into use only when the truth was subjected to such assaults as the latest ages and the ripest forms of unbelief would make upon it. Thus, in the several doctrines scattered here and there through the pages of Revelation, as if without special adjustment or even coherence, there is an underlying unity, a latent

cohesion, completeness, system, whose value as a proof of the divine authorship of the whole, even our age has hardly begun to appreciate. In like manner we are just learning to discern in the several books of Scripture—historic, biographic, poetical, preceptive in their contents, and separated widely in time and source and intent—a marvelous coalescence, harmony, oneness, which are compelling us to admit that, diverse as they are, they must have issued from a single mind, and a Mind Divine. So the testimony of prophecy, received at first only because they who uttered it seemed to be divinely commissioned for such disclosure of coming things, has been and is still being further verified to us by the amazing confirmations of history; and the barren sands of Tyre, and the desolate rocks of Edom, become to us, and to all ages, the mute witnesses to the accuracy of the predictions which foretold their righteous doom.

The most clear, touching, unquestionable among these testimonies—the one which most depends upon time for its exposition, and which in time gains the most convincing efficacy, is the living, maturing, conquering church of God on earth. Skeptics like Volney or Gibbon may point to the many vicissitudes of that church, and its conflicts and revulsions—to the corruption betrayed in some of its branches, and to the ceaseless strifes of part with part—to its decline or its feeble growth in many directions, and to its entire extinction in Northern Africa, and in Lesser Asia, where its seven candlesticks once shone as seven suns, and derisively say: What happens to other institutions will happen also to this. It has been subject to the same fluctuations; it embodies the same elements of weakness; it is under the same necessity of decay; and sooner or later, like the effete religions and empires of the Orient, this church must dwindle into extinction. Such are the hopes and the conclusions of unbelief—but are they warranted by the facts? Are the doctrines of this church growing less vital, convincing, precious? Is her experience degenerating from age to age, sinking gradually toward the low level of the ordinary life of man? Does time develop inherent weakness, fatal infirmities in the organization of the church, as in the constitutions and governments of mankind; and is her history, as we read it, suggestive of anything resembling declension or decay? Such conclusions are wholly unwarranted by the facts, when classified on the broadest scale, interpreted in the most philosophic method. These facts rather demonstrate the existence within that church of a supernatural quality or endowment which, while it does not deliver her wholly from the weakness incident to contact with human corruption, still effectually preserves her from that law of death which has passed upon all merely human organizations. The presence of this preservative and vitalizing agency renders invalid all skeptical reasoning from the decline of kingdoms, from the decay of false religions, from any phenomena observable in the fluctuating, variable, decaying life of the natural man. The prophecies of unbelief have not been, are never to be, transmuted into history. The church of God has existed and still exists, because its principles, spirit, operations, tendency are not of the earth. It still exists, and must continue to exist, because

God Himself dwells in it, and imparts to it His own perennial life.

Behold, therefore, what peculiar witness this supernatural church, thus living and growing from age to age, bears to the supernaturalness of the entire system in which it stands as a vital part. It is not reasoning in circles to say that, as the doctrine of God proves the church to be divine, so the church in turn demonstrates the divinity of the doctrine—that as the experience, organization, career of the church show it to be from God, so the church reflects a clear, persuasive light on these sources of its development, proving them also to have come from Him. As we reason from the system concerning the church, so we may fitly reason from the church concerning the entire system; and as we behold her, living through so many centuries, incorporating such a faith, exhibiting such a character, overcoming such hindrances, growing into such magnitude and beauty, and rising progressively into such pre-eminence among the institutions, influences, vital forces of the world, we may safely rest in the conviction that the holy religion, which is her light, her life, her glory, came from above.

2. We may also find in this central fact, the *verifying test of religious organizations, and the interpreting principle in the study of ecclesiastical history.* The most seductive plea now presented by the great masters of defense in the Papal Church—the argument which has won over to Rome such numbers from the ranks of ritualistic Episcopacy, and which is silently affecting many in other Protestant communions, is derived from historic sources; from the flavor of antiquity in its creeds

and institutions; from the dignity of its long suc-
cession of prelates and of holy rites; from the
massive strength consequent upon the accumula-
tions of time, and the wonderful unity, vitality,
effectiveness resulting from organizations perfected
through centuries of experience. A church like
this, robed in the antique purple of emperors, in-
heriting such treasures of the past, venerable and
yet bearing few traces of decrepitude, exhibiting
much of the vigor and skill of manhood, though
silvered with the white of ages, imposing as an organization, and most potent as an aggressive agency, may easily command the allegiance of minds
already belittled by playing with lawn and alb and
chasuble, and may even win the reverence of others
who are affected more by the carnal appearance,
than by the spiritual reality. But how unsatisfy-
ing do such considerations become, when brought
to a test more searching and more safe! Are these
manifestations supernatural — the beautiful and
strong and impressive product of the Spirit of God,
dwelling in the soul of man? Are these venerable
creeds the living expressions of the vital doctrines
of grace, now accepted and now embraced as the
very word of God; or are they the ornate caskets
in which that word lies hidden and ready for burial?
Are these forms of worship, these chanted hymns
and studied rites, and gorgeous demonstrations, the
truthful manifestations of a holy life, and a deep
experience of spiritual things; or only the artistic
delusions with which the natural heart strives to
calm its anxieties into repose? Are these amazing
exhibitions of vigorous activity, of sacrificing zeal,
of external growth and aggrandizement, the out-

ward signs of an inward communication with Christ, and of a complete and pure devotion to His cause; or simply the natural display of the spirit of party and the love of sect, apart from any deeper or more sacred feeling? In this vast, rich, strong, arrogant, aggrandizing organization, bearing the divine name, and retaining in its grasp many of the treasures and heritages of the true church of God, do we discern the presence of this supernatural quality, enlivening its doctrine, hallowing its experience, controlling in its constitution and its career? This is the conclusive test by which Romanism is yet to be measured; and this is the measurement by which Romanism is yet to be condemned.

Far in the opposite extreme we discern a multitude of other organizations, bearing indeed the name of the church of God, and claiming whatever prerogatives or honors that name may justify, yet liberalistic and rationalizing in their tendency, rejecting certain cardinal elements in the divine doctrine, doubting the reality of miracles and the teachings of prophecy, holding loose and destructive theories of inspiration, questioning the divinity of Jesus and the existence of the Holy Spirit, and thus practically throwing out of view that supernatural quality without which the church becomes nothing better than any human organism. Do not such bodies, in their very confessions, admit their own character, and write their own condemnation? If they are builded upon a denial and a lie—a denial of that truth of grace on which all other gracious truth reposes, and a lie concerning that central verity of religion, without which there can be no religion—what shall we say of them, but that they are in no sense or degree a part of that true church of God, in which His miraculous presence ever abides, as the Shekinah dwelt in His earliest tabernacle? If a divine Redeemer and a present Spirit and an inspired Word and a superhuman Life are held in question among them, or are covertly denied, then what are they but organizations of men, unworthy of fellowship, unworthy even of respect?

The true church of God, in distinction from such imitations, may be known by these conclusive tests. It may exist under different names, and with minor diversities in constitution and doctrine and worship; it may be found in various lands, and widely separated in its parts and members; it may be variously discerned in different ages, and its course in history may often seem dubious and defective. But wherever seen or studied, it may be instantly known as the one Holy and Catholic Church by these tests; an inspired Word, a spiritual Life, an indwelling Holy Ghost, an accepted, revered, enthroned Redeemer. Whatever names or minor characteristics it bears, in whatever land or age it may appear, these are the marks by which the true church may be known—these are the celestial signs by which it lives and conquers.

3. A third and final truth suggested by the fact we have considered, is *the essential oneness of this supernatural church,* notwithstanding whatever minor diversities may be apparent in it.

One of the most remarkable and propitious phenomena of the times is the rising aspiration after closer fellowship among the various bodies standing within the circle of evangelical Christianity. Denominations possessing in common the essential characteristics of the true church of God are, in these gracious days, becoming conscious that the points wherein they differ, are wholly subordinate to the divine verities in which they agree. Affinities in doctrine, affinities in polity, affinities in experience are assuming their just supremacy. The consciousness of a common work and of common dangers on the one side, and of common aims, hopes, destinies on the other, is drawing them together, just as the rising sentiment of patriotism excited by the stimulus of civil war, and growing under trial, is making of these many States one mighty, indivisible nation. Both rationalism and ritualism, the two great foes of a true supernaturalism, are contributing in various proportions to this grand result. The outlying sin and misery, both in Pagan and in Christian lands, are compelling genuine disciples of every name into community in labor, in sacrifice, in prayer. Different branches' of the Calvinistic stock are tracing their lineage beyond specific confessions and canons, to those remoter bases of scriptural truth on which they rest as a common foundation; and here they meet and mingle spontaneously with the advocates of that other great type of theology which, though at variance with Calvinism in many important features, yet deserves to be equally recognized as evangelical. Churches agreeing substantially in modes of government a. : seeking more intimate fellowship, sending the electric voice of cordial greeting across continents and oceans, and making the world melodious with the song of conscious and trustful brotherhood in Christ. And in all this who fails to discern, not simply some temporary gush of awakened sensibility, some popular current destined soon to cease, some partisan scheme devised in the mere mood of policy, but rather a divine movement, bone to his bone and flesh to his flesh, as in the valley of prophetic vision! Nay, who does not hope that these simultaneous awakenings to the loveliness and the law of spiritual brotherhood, are the bright dawning of that promised day when Zion shall arise in her true splendor, and shall conquer and possess the earth!

The principle underlying such fellowship is the principle we have considered—a supernatural unity in faith, in experience, in development. It may reveal itself in compacts on the basis of a kindred polity, but this can only be the prelude to something higher and more permanent. It may be shown in the adoption of common Confessions of Faith, but this must be simply the introduction to something still more momentous and precious. It may for a season be confined within the boundaries of states, the dividing courses of rivers or mountains, the shores of continents; but in the end it must overleap such barriers, and encompass and possess the earth. It may be defined by covenants, be placed under organic limitations, be unfolded amidst the zeal of party and the protest of sect, but at length it will triumph over these, and the earliest dream of the apostolic age will be verified in that one Holy and Catholic Church, whose boundaries are co-extensive with the earth, and whose duration extends to the end of the days of Millennial glory.

And what a conception is this, which thus shines down upon us, as the counterpart to it descended upon the gaze of the enraptured John! When the es

sential doctrines of the common Gospel shall be
eliminated from non-essential truth, and from philosophic interpretation—when the true experience
in Christ shall be distinguished from all other experience, and shall live and shine among men in its
celestial glory—when the organization and growth
of the church shall be in complete accordance with
its inner spirit, and that church shall stand forth
among men as the first of human institutions, the
kingdom of kingdoms, the divine family, the ordained home of the soul; how will the splendor of
that church become as the light of seven suns, and
her glory fill and illuminate the earth! This has been
the dream of prophecy from the beginning of time
—this has been the hope of true believers from Abraham until now—this is the song and the expecta-
tion of all true saints in our day, and in every age.
And in due season, in the progress of His providence,
in the fullness of His grace, God will doubtless turn
these dreams to facts, these hopes to realities, this
expectant song into the anthem of universal praise.

FATHERS AND BRETHREN: I accept for myself, without reserve and without hesitation, the cardinal verity which I have been engaged in defining and illustrating, together with whatever of truth or of duty
may be included therein. I rejoice not merely to
live in the inspiration of this blessed reality, but also
to be made, in the place this day assigned me, an
instrument in its scientific unfolding and defense.
In this sacred Institution, founded on the doctrine
I have been enforcing, and from foundation to turret
consecrated to the support of the true and living
church of God, I now give my life unreservedly to
this vast, difficult, solemn, precious service; com-

mitting myself to your sympathy and favor, and commending my work unto Him whom we all accept as Master.   And may He, who has thus condescended to reveal Himself to men supernaturally, in and by His church, lead us all through her tasks and her nurture to that bright world where whatever is natural merely is lost to view, and where that church is fully manifested as the supernatural body of Him who filleth all in all.

DISCOURSE.

My anticipations of this hour, and my view of the work to which it introduces me, have fixed my attention upon *the Relations of Christian Truth to Christian Life.* This is, therefore, the theme to which I respectfully invite the attention of my hearers: the truth which is revealed, by divine inspiration, in the Holy Scriptures; the life which each regenerate soul lives by faith in the Son of God, and which animates and energizes His body, the church: the relations which these sustain to each other.

Not aiming to exhaust so extensive a subject in so short a time as I may properly occupy, I limit myself to the consideration of it in three aspects, viz.: Christian truth in its relations to Christian experience, to Christian activity, and to Christian liberty.

I. We consider first, *the Relations of Christian Truth to Christian Experience.*

We here have in view the effect which the truth produces upon the spiritual condition of those who believingly receive it. This is comprehensively exhibited in that remarkable prayer of our Lord for them whom God had given Him—for the disciples then present and hearing, and for all who should afterward believe in Him through their word. "Sanctify them through thy truth: thy word is truth."

Sanctification, as we understand the Holy Scriptures to teach, is something more than mere innocence or blamelessness. That may be predicated of creatures quite incapable of positive virtue. Beautifully is it ascribed to the dove and the lamb, whose sweet harmlessness God has honored by making them types of His incarnate Son and of the Holy Spirit. Tenderly do we recognize it in those human beings whose imbecility divests them, as we suppose, of accountability. I know of no more touching and graceful euphemism, in human speech, than one calling such persons "*innocents.*"

Surely mere innocence, depending on incapacity for guilt, is a wholly different thing from scriptural sanctification, as we believe that our Confession of Faith and our Catechism truly define it.

We might also conceive of comparative innocence—perhaps even of absolute innocence, depending on the lack of opportunity to sin, or upon exemption from temptation—which would be no fulfillment of the scriptural idea. Human innocence such as could have been preserved by effectually fencing the tempter out of Eden, or by leaving the human pair nothing to desire, or by divesting them of every susceptibility through which temptation could approach their will—such innocence was not what God would have. Not to that does His gracious work of sanctification restore us. What He values is character, positive virtue—not mere negative blamelessness. It was exemplified in the second Adam, who doubtless possessed all human susceptibilities in perfection, and had them severely tried in a protracted conflict with the prince of evil. He "was in all points tempted like as we are, yet without sin."

It is to this positive, Christ-like virtue that scriptural sanctification brings us. True Christian experience has its proper result in the production of Christian character. It is not a mere washing, though it muśt be that first of all; but it is also a nurture, a discipline, a training, an upbuilding.

"The grace of God that bringeth salvation," (σωτήριος) is a grace "teaching us"—(*i. e.* educating us, παιδέvουσα) "that denying ungodliness and worldly lusts, we should live soberly, righteously, and godly, in this present world." Sanctification is "the work of God's free grace," but it is God "working in us to will and to do of His good pleasure." God's sanctifying work within us effectuates our working out of our own salvation.

Our Confession of Faith rightly affirms this divine work to be "throughout in the whole man." It reaches to all the elements of character, and to all the developments of life. It has to do with the positive side of charactèr as truly and as much as with the negative side. It is manifested in restraining us from wrong-doing, no more than in prompting us and strengthening us unto well-doing. It no more produces meekness, and gentleness, and patience, and purity, than courage, fortitude, and holy energy. If it subdues the wild turbulence of nature into submission aṇd teachableness and trust, which will love to sit at the feet of Jesus, and will

be fit to lean on His breast, it equally rouses from
the indolence of nature, or assumes the direction
and control of native vehemence, and makes its
possessors the Boanerges of Christian history.

With this idea of God's work of sanctification in
the hearts of believers, we are prepared to see how
He accomplishes it by means of His truth, the truth
of His word. He has so constituted the human
mind, that it is capable of apprehending spiritual
truth, and of being essentially affected by it. Herein is the creature, man, distinguished from all the
creatures below him, and herein is he assimilated
to all the created intelligences above him, and to
the Creator Himself.

The truth which Christ came into the world to
testify, the truth of God's holy word, surely no
creature below man is capable of receiving. Man
is, God has made him so. The great characteristic
truths of the Bible can be received by every sane,
mature human mind. Its most essential truths can
be received by every attentive and teachable child,
at a very early age, received too with all their sanctifying efficacy. This is a glorious distinction of our
human nature, to be thoughtfully kept in mind, not
thanklessly forgotten. The mind's ability to be *influenced* by the truth is more than its power to apprehend it. There are truths which no human mind
can apprehend, can know and contemplate, and re-
main as it were before. When a human mind gets the
idea of God, learns, knows that He is, and apprehends
something of His greatness and excellence, it must
be influenced by that truth. There must then be
suitable affections toward God, and so the developments of a good character, or else there will be un-

suitable affections toward Him, and so the development of a bad character. The same will continue to be true of every increment of religious knowledge which the soul may attain, in respect to the being of God, His character, His works, His ways, His word. The harmony of the created mind with the truth of God will evermore be its perfection. Its variance from that truth, its repugnance to it, its disobedience* will ever be the marring and deterioration of its character.

In God's gracious work upon the renewed soul, in His nurture and bringing to perfection of the new spiritual life which He has supernaturally originated, He acts in conformity with the constitution of the soul, as He originally established it. He uses the truth to sanctify it—His own truth—His own word. Increasing knowledge of the objects brought to view in His word, with the exercise of suitable affections toward them; increasing knowledge of His law and growing conformity to it; increasing knowledge of the principles and methods of His grace, with submission of the heart to them; deepening knowledge of sin and growing aversion to it; progress in self-knowledge, and consequent increase of humility; increasing knowledge of Christ and consequent increase of confidence in Him; increasing knowledge of the person and work of the Holy Spirit, and corresponding increase of willing and obedient subjection to His gracious influence and guidance—this is sanctification. In no aspect does

---

* Aπειθεια—See how the idea of UNBELIEF blends with that of DISOBEDIENCE in the etymology of this scriptural term; and how naturally in scripture phrase THE TRUTH is made the object of the verb to OBEY. Gal. v. 7.

this process appear to be possible apart from the truth, as it is revealed to us in the Holy Scriptures. Certainly God has not revealed, and has not appointed any other method of sanctification.

We may carry our view farther back, to the very beginning of the Christian life, to the new birth itself. An apostle tells us, that God "of His own will begat us, *with the word of truth;*" and all apostles, and all evangelical preachers after them, evidently relied upon the preaching of the word, as the appointed means through which to procure the regeneration of souls, by the power of the Holy Spirit.

Such are the relations of Christian truth to Christian experience, from its inception at the new birth, onward through all the stages of its advancement, unto heavenly perfection. Divine truth is its element. Religious experience which is not conformed to God's word, and nourished by it, is not Christian experience. The Spirit of God does not work in the hearts of men, contrary to the truth which He has revealed to the minds of men. Religious experience which, in any degree, disregards scriptural truth, is so far spurious, is so far morbid. Its fervors are fevers; its growth is inflation; its raptures are delirium.

We have one of the sweet proofs that we are truly born again, when we, "as new-born babes desire the sincere milk of the word;" nor can we prosperously "grow in grace," except as we grow "in the knowledge of our Lord and Savior Jesus Christ," for this purpose searching the Scriptures which testify of Him.

II. *The Relations of Christian Truth to Christian Activity.*

Genuine Christian experience affects all the powers of the man. Spiritual religion, experienced within the heart, will find outward manifestation. A sanctified heart will put forth holy activity as certainly as a depraved heart will put forth sinful activity. The man or the woman who loves Christ will work for Him. Whoever trusts in Christ for salvation, will desire to be engaged in His service. In proportion as the church is filled with the Holy Spirit, it will abound in labors for advancing the kingdom of God in the world.

How shall this spontaneous activity of regenerate nature be rightly directed? Where shall it find its rule? How shall it secure itself from becoming zeal without knowledge, and occasioning the profitless waste or harmful misdirection of energy?

The obvious answer is—"God's written word must direct us." Yet we cannot find in the Bible specific directions for every actually occuring occasion; we cannot look into the Bible to determine what our duty is, as we look into the dictionary to learn the orthography or pronunciation of a word. The Book of God was meant for wider use, and for more comprehensive instruction than that. It has indeed many specific directions; but it abounds in the inculcation of principles of wide and various application. He does not truly know the Holy Scriptures, who has not thoroughly digested their teachings into an orderly system, giving them their true relations, and revealing their real harmony—a harmony which can be manifested in a consistent

Christain life. The church is using her power healthfully and to truly beneficial ends, only as she is rightly instructed out of God's word, and, led by the Spirit, conforms her activity to its teachings.

We are living in a time of extraordinary activity. This is true of secular forces and movements; and it is equally true of the spiritual forces and religious movements, which belong to the kingdom of Christ. Abundant are the efforts to extend the church—to evangelize the masses—to make the means of grace attractive and effective—to adapt the preaching of the gospel and all evangelistic instrumentalities to the various situations, and circumstances, and habits of the people. There is a great awakening of the mind of the church to the duty of making the way of salvation known to all mankind; and there is unprecedented earnestness in devising and applying methods for pressing its claims upon their attention. This is doubtless one of the most hopeful signs of the times,—the more so, inasmuch as the animating principle of this earnestness appears to be simple evangelical faith. "*Justification by faith*" is its leading idea. "*Come to Jesus*," is its continual call. "*Christ crucified*," is all its hope.

It is of incalculable importance that this movement be kept pure and scriptural; that it be not perverted by erroneous views of the plan of salvation; that it be not corrupted by the infusion of unscriptural elements. Is it certain that it will not be? Has the enemy ever failed to find opportunity to sow tares in such rich fields, or has he ever neglected to embrace his opportunity? Has he not always been ready and eager to mislead human minds, when roused to such earnestness, into ruinous errors? Do we not, as always heretofore, so now also, need the scriptural caution: "Be sober, be vigilant, because your adversary, the devil, as a roaring lion, walketh about, seeking whom he may devour?"

How shall the people of God, especially the converts won by these evangelistic labors, be guarded against the evils of a perverted and corrupted faith? The ready answer will be—"By the Word of God;—by giving them a more comprehensive and more thorough knowledge of the Holy Scriptures." It is not enough, that copies of the Bible are multiplied, and cheapened, and distributed. We must get them read. There must be earnest, thorough, comprehensive study of the Bible. The minds of men must be made to receive and to hold the system of truth which it contains. There is a system of truth contained in the Bible, and it is as evidently wise and useful to possess ourselves of it in a considerate, orderly, scientific way, as it is to acquire, in that way, any sort of secular knowledge. It is as obviously unwise and unsafe to content ourselves with fragmentary, desultory, disjointed views of Christian truth, as of any department of natural science, or of any branch of secular business by which you propose to serve your generation, and gain your livelihood. The evangelistic activity and enterprise of the people of God, so hopefully characteristic of this age, as much needs the regulation, and the upholding, and the safeguard of true theological science, as the effective operating of the magnetic telegraph and of steam-power need the support and regulation of physical science; as much as commercial enterprise needs the basis of really scientific knowledge of the laws of trade—of the relations of demand and supply—of the principles which must ultimately rule in the production, distribution and consumption of commodities—the whole science of political economy.

The church must take care, by her pulpits, and her literature, and her schools, to conserve and defend and inculcate a sound, scriptural theology—an orderly, consistent (*i. e.*, a truly *scientific*) system of doctrine; or else her abundant activity will soon bring her into the condition into which a belligerent nation would be brought by closing all her armories, and sending all her skilled artisans to the field.

III. *The Relations of Christian Truth to Christian Liberty.*

Nothing is more evident than that those religious systems which enslave the people, do not enlighten the people. Their motto is: "Ignorance is the mother of devotion." Blind, unquestioning, unthinking acceptance of the church's dogmas, and unresisting subjection to hierarchical authority, is their highest form of piety. The chains of such spiritual despotism have been broken only by those minds into which the truth of God's word has come, with its quickening, energizing power. They have experienced the fulfillment of that word of Christ— "Ye shall know the truth, and the truth shall make you free." The instrument whereby God purifies the soul from its pollution, is the same with which He delivers it from its bondage. The more correctly and thoroughly any mind understands and knows

the truth, as it is revealed in the Bible, the more incapable is it of slavish subjection to any creature,
to any human authority.

When Luther had received into his heart the divine assurance, " *The just shall live by his faith*,"
when he had tasted the sweetness and felt the efficacy of that truth in his personal experience,
delivering him from the burden and the taint of
personal guilt, he soon found it lifting him up to a
stature and a vigor of heroic manhood. These words
resounding in his heart, as he kneeled abjectly on
"Pilate's stair-case," caused him to start up amazed
and ashamed of the degrading superstition. This
truth mightily working in his soul, solemnly and
prayerfully meditated, thoroughly and devoutly
studied, in its various relations and consequences,
bore the reformer forward in all his work and conflicts, until he could stand in the presence of the
assembled principalities and powers, the most for-
midable array before which a confessor in that age
could be called to plead, and could calmly answer
the demand to retract his honest and conscientious
utterances, thus—"Since your Serene Majesty and
your High Mightinesses require of me a simple, clear,
and direct answer, I will give one, and it is this:—I
cannot submit my faith either to the Pope or to the
Councils, because it is as clear as noonday that
they have often fallen into error, and even into
glaring inconsistency with themselves. If then I
am not convinced by proof from Holy Scripture or
by cogent reasons; if I am not satisfied by the very
texts that I have cited; and if my judgment is not
in this way brought into subjection to God's word,
I neither can nor will retract anything; for it can-

not be right for a Christian to speak anything against his conscience. * * * * * I stand here, and can say no more:—*God help me*, AMEN." It is the courage that can stand and look into the fiery center of extremest peril, and will not flee.

The same was sublimely exemplified, fifteen hundred years before, by those unlearned and illiterate men, who "had been with Jesus," when they said to the threatening Jewish Council: "We cannot but speak the things which we have seen and heard." This is no native courage, no human heroism. It is the admirable efficacy of the Word of God, lifting the soul above every other fear, by filling it with the fear of displeasing Him by unfaithfulness to His word, which He "hath magnified above all His name."

Similar fidelity to the truth, exemplified, not by a few eminent leaders, but by "the noble army of martyrs" and confessors, has achieved and secured all the true and precious liberty which we have inherited. It also, and it alone, preserves true Christian liberty from degenerating into unchristian license. Liberty *in* God's word—freedom from all human dogmatism—is broadly distinguished from liberty to reject God's word, or to exalt human reason above it.

Our own times are not free from dangers to Christian liberty. The spirit of dogmatism and of arrogant ecclesiasticism has not ceased to menace it on the one hand; and the spirit of irreverent speculation and ungodly liberalism has dug a more perilous gulf for it on the other. To the Christians of this generation, as to those of other days, this sacred trust is committed, with the augmented sacredness which so glorious a history has gathered. Peculiar and awful is the responsibility of those to whom the church gives exemption from secular pursuits, and time, and means of support, and books, and teachers, and then the most affecting bestowal of her generous confidence, setting them apart, and setting them upon her high places, to be the ever watchful and faithful defenders of her faith—of the truth in all its solemn and vital relations to her glorious liberty, her noble work, and her heavenly life.

Brethren, let us recognize this responsibility, and may God enable us to fulfill it.

Trustees and Alumni of Lane Theological Seminary:—Half a year ago, while I was occupied with the cares and labors of a most precious pastoral charge, your election officially communicated, and your arguments and solicitations spontaneously and numerously presented, called me to the office in which I have now been inaugurated. The call was convincingly evidenced to my conscience as from the Lord, and I dared not disobey it. Sincere and serious misgivings in regard to my fitness and preparation for this place and this work, did not release me from that conviction. Assured of your generous confidence and fraternal co-operation, and relying upon that Divine help which surely will not be denied to our united prayers, I am here to enter upon the work thus assigned to me, solemnly consecrating to it whatever powers I may possess, and whatever acquirements diligent study may enable me to make. I expect increasingly to find and to feel the inadequacy of both.

I have comfort in the assurance that my general

view of what ought to be attempted here is in harmony with the views of the brethren having charge of the other departments of instruction, and with your own; in harmony also, I believe, with the views and the life of him, so highly honored and so sincerely loved by you all, who having worthily fulfilled the career which God assigned him here, now patiently waits for the call to come and receive the "crown of righteousness" which doubtless is laid up for him.

The assigning of Systematic and Pastoral Theology to one instructor (which was done by the Trustees without consulting me), significantly intimates your estimate of those Relations between Christian Truth and Christian Life, upon which we have meditated. You have made it my official duty to teach Theology, scientifically indeed, yet not apart from its practical bearings and uses. You doubtless believe that that Theology is most truly scientific, which most clearly evidences itself as Biblical; and that that is the same, which can be carried most effectively into the pulpit, and into all the various and solemn work and care of the pastor. Fully concurring with you in this view, I can only promise to give my best endeavors to the realization of it.

Students of Lane Seminary: In the department of Systematic and Pastoral Theology, you will be invited not so much to sit at the feet of a teacher, as to accompany a fellow-disciple, in searching the Holy Scriptures, that you may learn from them, and become "able to teach others also," "what man is to believe concerning God, and what duty God requires of man." I shall deem it my duty, not authoritatively to determine your belief, but fraternally to help your inquiries. We will sit together at the feet of the Master. We will search together the Holy Scriptures which testify of Him. We will seek together the illumination of the Spirit of Truth. We will try to remember always, that He does not enlighten unless He also purifies. Therefore we will ever unite with all our fellow Christians in offering up, for ourselves and for them, our Lord's own prayer for us — "*Sanctify us through thy truth.*"

Historical Sketch.

THE conviction and the hope in which LANE THE-
OLOGICAL SEMINARY had its origin, were well expressed
by the venerated Dr. Beecher in his letter to the
Board of Trustees, written in 1831, while he was
considering the question of his transfer from Boston
to the Professorship of Theology in the Institution :
" The work of providing an evangelical ministry
for the West *must be done chiefly at the West.* The
East cannot furnish the requisite number of students,
nor the funds to educate them; and if she could, it
were better that the ministry of the West should
be indigenous (native) rather than imported. As
an ally, the Atlantic States may do and are willing
to do much. But it is the sons of the West, *educated on her own soil*, who must preach the gospel to
the West; and in the great work of educating such
a ministry, the Lane Seminary may, if prospered,
exert an important influence."

It was this view which led the brothers LANE, na-
tives of Maine, but at the time engaged in business
at New Orleans, to resolve, early in the year 1828,
to set apart "one thousand dollars per annum, for
four years, and a fourth of their annual income
thereafter," for the founding of an Institution at
some point in the West, " the primary object of
which should be to educate pious young men for

the Gospel Ministry." The elder brother, being in
the Baptist connection, shortly afterward came to
Cincinnati for the purpose of selecting a location
and starting the enterprise, primarily under the
auspices of that denomination. Discovering that
his plan could not be carried out in that form, and
learning that some preliminary steps had been
taken toward the establishment of a Presbyterian
Seminary at this point, he was led to make his generous proposal to those especially interested in that
movement. The proposal was accepted, and in October, 1828, a Board of Trustees was organized, and
the noble enterprise was fairly undertaken.

The charter, which was granted by the Legisla-
ture of Ohio, in February, 1829, conferred upon the
Institution all the prerogatives of a college or uni-
versity, as well as those of a theological seminary.
For several years, academic as well as professional
instruction was afforded to students, but in 1835
this department was finally discontinued. It was
also provided that some amount of manual labor
should be required from each student, at the dis-
cretion of the Board of Trust; but after several
years of experiment, this feature in the plan was
likewise abandoned. Regular instruction in Theology was commenced in 1832, and, subsequently to
1835, the work of the Institution was limited to
this department exclusively.

The donation of the brothers LANE, was followed
by the gift in 1829, of sixty acres of land, bestowed
by members of the KEMPER family, then resident on
Walnut Hills—a gift increased in 1832, by a permanent lease of fifty additional acres, granted by Mr.
ELNATHAN KEMPER, an intelligent and earnest friend

of the new enterprise. This donation not only determined at the first the specific location of the Seminary, but subsequently became, and still continues to be, the chief source of its income and support. Steps were taken, as soon as the charter was obtained, to procure an additional endowment such as would enable the Institution to perform the work for which it had been established. A subscription of nearly $5,000 was secured in Cincinnati and the vicinity, chiefly for the purpose of erecting suitable buildings; but all efforts to procure funds from more distant sources proved abortive. Late in 1830, when Dr. Beecher was called to his place in the Institution, a more vigorous and successful attempt was made. Upon condition of his acceptance, $20,000 were subscribed by ARTHUR TAPPAN, Esq., and a further sum of $30,000 was pledged by other friends of the enterprise at Philadelphia and New York and elsewhere. To secure these pledges, about $16,000 were raised in 1832 at the West, and during the three succeeding years, the resources of the Seminary were considerably increased by further donations from persons in the East, whose hearts had been enlisted in the great work of providing an educated ministry for the valley of the Mississippi.

During this period, the Chapel, Dormitory, and Boarding Hall, and also two dwellings for Professors were erected, at a cost of nearly $50 000. The Library was procured at an expense varying but little from $10,000. Productive funds were invested to the amount of $25,000; and the annual income from this source, and from rented lands, was largely increased by the interest on the TAPPAN en-

dowment, and on other unpaid subscriptions. The
pecuniary prospects of the Institution at this point
were highly favorable; but the financial revulsion
of 1837, and the succeeding years, rendered Mr.
TAPPAN and many other subscribers unable to pay
either principal or interest on their pledges, and
reduced the pecuniary resources of the Seminary
to the slight income from rented lands, and the interest of the scant endowment already in hand.

In other respects the Institution had been well
furnished for its predestined work. Dr. BEECHER
was inducted into office, as Professor of Systematic
Theology, on the twenty-sixth of December, 1832,
and on the same day, Dr. THOMAS J. BIGGS, elected in
1831, entered upon his duties as Professor of Ecclesiastical History and Church Polity. In July, 1833,
CALVIN E. STOWE, D. D., elected in the preceding
year, began his work in the department of Biblical
Literature. In 1835, BAXTER DICKINSON, D. D., was
installed as Professor of Sacred Rhetoric and Pastoral Theology, and occupied that position till the
fall of 1839, when Dr. BIGGS and himself were constrained by the pecuniary straits of the Institution
to resign. Dr. DICKINSON was succeeded in October,
1840, by Dr. ALLEN, prior to that time a Professor in
Marietta College; and the duties of Dr. BIGGS were
assumed chiefly by Professor STOWE.

During this period the Seminary, notwithstanding its great financial embarrassment, had reached
the point of assured success and of extensive usefulness. For the five years previous to 1840, during
which it had been devoted exclusively to theological instruction, the classes had averaged about
twenty; and from the beginning to that date more

than one hundred young men had here received some degree of preparation for the ministerial work.

The succeeding decade, which closed with the resignation of Dr. BEECHER and Professor STOWE in the summer of 1850, was also a period of marked success, though characterized by much of trial and sacrifice on the part of those to whom the work of instruction had been intrusted. Not far from two hundred and twenty-five students were connected with the Institution during this period; and among the graduates were many whose earnest and sucsessful labors in the missionary churches of the West and on heathen shores, fully verified the hopes cherished by those who had founded the Institution. They had been both called into the ministry through its influence, and trained for the ministry by its practical culture; and their work testified, and still testifies, to its inestimable worth as an agency tributary to the kingdom of Christ.

The resignations just mentioned were followed in 1851, by the transfer of Dr. ALLEN to the chair of Systematic Theology, and the election of J. B. CONDIT, D. D., to fill the vacancy thus occasioned, and of Professor GEORGE E. DAY to the place vacated by Dr. STOWE. Three years later Dr. CONDIT was constrained by ill health to resign his position, and in 1855, Rev. HENRY SMITH, D. D., then President of Marietta College, was elected to the vacated Professorship, instruction in Church History being also assigned to him. Upon the resignation of Dr. SMITH in 1862, to accept a pastoral charge, Rev. LLEWELYN J. EVANS was called to the department of Church History. In 1866, Dr. SMITH was again elected to the chair of Sacred Rhetoric, and the same year, Professor DAY tendered his resignation, and was succeeded by Rev. ELISHA BALLANTINE, In the following year, Dr. ALLEN was compelled by declining health to seek release from active service, and was made Professor Emeritus ; and Rev. HENRY A. NELSON, D. D., then of St. Louis, was chosen to be his successor. Dr. BALLANTINE also resigning, Professor EVANS was transferred to that department, and Rev. E. D. MORRIS, D. D., of Columbus, Ohio, was elected to the chair of Ecclesiastical History and Church Polity.

After the original effort for the founding and endowment of the Seminary, which was ended in 1836, nothing was done for more than twenty years to increase its resources, excepting through the progressive renting of the KEMPER lands. But in 1858 it became evident that some additional means of income must be secured, or the Institution must be closed. A new Library building, and an enlargement of the Library itself had become indispensable. The other structures, erected mostly thirty years previously, were in imperative need of repairs. The Seminary was largely indebted to its self-denying Faculty; and this debt was annually accumulating. An increase of the Endowment Fund was an unavoidable necessity, unless indeed the enterprise should for a season be suspended. In this exigency, an earnest appeal was made to the churches of the West, and this appeal was followed by a strenuous effort, which resulted in the discharge of the impending indebtedness, in the erection of an excellent Library Hall through the liberality of a single donor, and in a considerable increase of the Endowment Fund. A little later, through the liberality of another friend, a large addition was made to the Library, and a good foundation was laid for a permanent Fund, to be used in further enlargement.

The income from lands has increased largely within a few years, but not in a ratio commensurate with the wants of the Institution; and the income from this source has now nearly reached its maximum. A liberal bequest of $10,000 to the Endowment Fund, together with an additional bequest of $5,000 for the support of students and for other purposes, has recently been made to the Seminary, by one whose mind and heart had been deeply interested in the work of preparing young men for the ministry. Other Scholarship Funds have been received from time to time, amounting in the aggregate to several thousands of dollars, and the avails of a considerable legacy, left in trust for the education of a Western ministry, are also, in part, applied by the legatees to this purpose, in connection with this Institution.

During what may be termed the second period in its history, extending from the resignation of Dr. BEECHER to the present time, the Seminary has continued, often amid very serious embarrassments, to contribute much to the object for which it was instituted. About one hundred and eighty young men have here received, in part or wholly, their special training for the ministerial work; and most of these are now actively engaged in that work, mainly in the West. A very large proportion of the churches of our denomination, and many in other denominations, in Ohio and Indiana, and the other States lying between the Alleghanies and the Mississippi, have thus been supplied with the preaching of the Word. Though limited by scant resources, and unfurnished in other respects with the requisite equipments, the Institution has thus in its later, as in its earlier career, achieved results in which the hearts of its friends may ever rejoice.

This judgment is confirmed by a survey of the entire history of the Seminary, extending through a third of a century. It was planted as a very small seed. It has been but very imperfectly nurtured or sustained. Its resources have never been adequate to its needs, and have been altogether inferior to those of other Institutions attempting the same work. It has labored and struggled on in silence, and yet with the Divine blessing. Its corps of instructors have been as competent, efficient, successful, as they have been patient, toilsome, self-denying. Its influence has been widely and deeply felt among the churches of the Mississippi Valley. It has called many into the ministry, who without it would have been engaged in some secular calling. It has gathered within its walls between four and five hundred students whom it has instructed faithfully, not simply in the principles of a sound theology, but also in the exercise of those spiritual qualities and graces which alone can make men competent to proclaim Christ to a dying world.

The Statistical Records of the New School Presbyterian Church, for 1867, show that *one hundred and eighty*, or about *one in ten* of the ministers now in that connection, have been educated in part or wholly at LANE. Some of these are laboring in foreign lands; a few are in the Eastern or Middle

States, but the vast majority are toiling in the Missionary fields of the West, from the Alleghanies onward to Nevada and California. In Ohio there are *fifty-five;* in Indiana *thirty-eight;* in Illinois *twenty-four;* in Michigan *fifteen;* and in the aggregate we find that more than *one* in *five* of the ministry of this denomination in the West have been students in this Seminary. Yet these constitute *less than one-half* of the number who have here been trained for the sacred office. Many have passed from their work to their reward; and scores of others are found in other branches of the Presbyterian family, in the Congregational and Baptist Churches, and in the Methodist, the Episcopal, and the Lutheran connections. Who can estimate how vast a work these representatives of LANE have wrought; or how much the cause of Evangelical religion in the Mississippi Valley is indebted to their sacrifices, their labors, their prayers!

In surveying such a history and work, and in looking at the present position and prospects of this beloved Seminary, we have great reason to thank God and take courage. The past has been noble and full of precious fruitage. The present, also, is in a high degree propitious. The Institution is again blessed with an earnest, harmonious, competent Faculty; composed of brethren who at great sacrifice have accepted their several positions, because they believe the maintenance of LANE to be indispensable to the continued life and prosperity of our Western churches, and who are resolved by the grace of God to emulate the labor and patience and devotion of those who have preceded them in these high posts of service. The students now con-

nected with the Seminary, though few in numbers,
are more than content with the privileges afforded
them; and are devoting themselves happily to that
thorough and practical study which alone can make
the efficient minister. Assurances of confidence and
of sympathy are freely extended to the Institution
on every hand; and so far as we can observe, its
prospects for effective usefulness, as an agency tributary to the kingdom of Christ in the West, are in
the highest degree encouraging.

The present pecuniary condition of the Seminary,
is admirably presented in the accompanying statement of the Treasurer. The income from leased
lands, and rented buildings, and from the Endowment Fund, the form and the amount of the Scholarship and Library Funds, the character of the
several investments, the annual expenditure, etc.,
may here be seen at a glance. To this staement
there should be added, in a full estimate of the
material resources of the Institution, the Seminary
campus, consisting of nearly ten acres, beauifully
situated just outside of the limits of Cincinnai; on
which are located the Chapel, the Library, th Dormitory, and the Boarding Hall, furnishing—when
suitably repaired—a complete equipment ii this
regard for all purposes contemplated in the nsti-
tution.

WHAT IS NOW NEEDED, in order to render all hese
resources more productive, and to qualify the Seminary thoroughly for still larger and better wck, is
an early increase of its pecuniary resources. It is
indispensable that the Boarding Hall, recently rendered worthless by fire, should be immediately re-
built; and this work is now progressing at amn-

ticipated expense of $18,000. It is almost as important that the Dormitory, erected thirty years ago, should be completely repaired—made a pleasant and convenient home for those congregated in it. It is very desirable that our grounds, made beautiful by nature, should be properly improved; and that one or two additional dwellings for Professors should ere long be erected. Additional provision must soon be made for instruction in Hebrew, and by special courses of lectures, and as will be seen by the Report of the Treasurer, the present inadequacy of the income to meet the current expenditures, to say nothing of these additional needs, will require a considerable increase of the Endowment Fund.

To MEET THIS NECESSITY, the Board of Trustees have resolved to raise, as soon as practicable, the sum of $100,000; which sum they deem sufficient to supply these various wants, and to place the Seminary in a position of independence and of usefulness for a generation to come. As a proof of their convictions respecting the importance and worth of the Institution, and of their personal faith in its future, and in the blessing of God upon it, they have themselves—although nearly half of the Endowment of 1858, was contributed by them—subscribed *one-third of this amount;* and, having done their personal duty, they now appeal to brethren of like faith and convictions, to aid them in obtaining the remainder. The considerations on which such an appeal must be based, are substantially these:

1. Theological Seminaries are, in our age and country, indispensable adjuncts to an intelligent, earnest, developing Christianity. Without their aid, all other agencies for the diffusion of the Gos-

pel become ineffectual. While this is becoming the experience of all evangelical denominations in our land, it is specially the experience of such as are Calvinistic and Presbyterian.

2. The geographical distribution of such Seminaries, in a denomination aspiring like ours to be national in extent and influence, is not only desirable, but indispensable. Such an Institution, planted in any given region, becomes in many ways a living, potent, effectual call to the ministry, and an inestimable fountain of blessing to the surrounding churches. The distribution of such Institutions, within appropriate limits, not only contributes to the highest development of denominational life in every part, but also secures a due representation of doctrinal variety, and the largest measure of both liberality and comprehensiveness in the exposition of the True Faith.

3. A Theological Seminary is needed by our denomination at the West, where more than half of our churches are located, and where the largest part of our denominational work during the present generation is to be done. It were useless to expect the East to supply a ministry for the West—were this practicable, it would for many reasons be undesirable. "As an ally, the Atlantic States may do, and are willing to do much. But it is—as Dr BEECHER has said—the sons of the West, educated on her own soil, who must preach the Gospel to the West."

4. The present and prospective necessities of the West are exceedingly urgent. More than two hundred churches of our denomination, in this vast region, are now unsupplied with pastors, and many of

them are already perishing from spiritual hunger. The wide field for Missionary effort is growing wider year by year; and the demand for an educated ministry is constantly increasing. These urgent necessities, even our utmost endeavor cannot fully meet.

5. Lane Theological Seminary was never established as a local or provincial Institution; but rather was intended to be, as far as our denomination is concerned, a source of supply for the entire West. We have accepted, and still do accept, this vast and destitute region as our field, and are determined by Divine grace, so to furnish and equip the Seminary, that it shall be competent to do all the work which God may assign it, within the whole territory where He has planted it.

6. This is the only Theological Seminary of our denomination now existing, or likely soon to be established, in the West. The time will probably arrive when others may be needed; but whatever work in this department is done now, or for years to come, must be done by LANE. The vast responsibility is laid for the present on this single Institution; and so far as these enormous destitutions are soon met, the supplies must emanate chiefly from this source.

7. The location of our Seminary is highly advantageous. Though too far South to be entirely convenient to the remoter Northwest, it is yet by hundreds of miles nearer to the farthest extreme than any other Institution; and the numerous lines of railway now centering at Cincinnati, make it accessible, cheaply, from any point. On the other side, the Seminary is exactly in the central latitude of the general territory which we desire as a denom-

ination to possess; and the changing parallels of
commerce, trending more and more toward the South
and Southwest, will soon open to its influence the
entire Mississippi Valley from the Lakes to the Gulf.

8. The Seminary already possesses, at a low estimate, $150,000 of productive funds, and an invest-
ment in grounds and buildings of at least equal
value. This large accumulation only needs such an
addition as we propose to secure, to render it remu-
nerative in a far higher ratio. Such an income
would make the present investment far more fruit-
ful, and would remove every present restriction of
a pecuniary nature, upon the widest usefulness of
the Institution.

9. Once endowed and furnished, according to our
plan, the Seminary will probably continue for a
generation, and perhaps for ages, to do its allotted
work without further assistance. Experience justifies the hope, that henceforth the private charities of
intelligent Christians, conferred either during life,
or by bequest, will be adequate to meet all its prospective and developing wants.

10. The present necessities, especially in the line
of improved grounds and buildings, will appeal
primarily to the citizens of Cincinnati, who are interested in the beautifying of these already unsur-
passed suburbs, and whose local pride may properly
be enlisted in the complete endowment of the Seminary. But we have believed that Christian men of
our denomination, throughout the West and Northwest, would feel the force of the broader considerations suggested, and would share with us in an
effort which appeals to their convictions and sym-
pathies equally with ours. We have trusted that

such brethren at the East would appreciate our views and our hopes, and would assist us in an undertaking which is for the benefit, not of the West alone, but of the whole land, and of the world.

It is more than thirty years since assistance has been solicited for LANE from the East, and with the exception of the limited subscription of 1858, nothing has been contributed by the West since the founding of the Institution. The present generation of Christians in our denomination have never had the opportunity of expressing their sympathy with our beloved Seminary, and their appreciation of the work it has done, and is still striving to do. Surely an appeal will not be made to them in vain.

Perhaps it should be added that in the event of *reunion*, while the sphere of the Seminary may be geographically limited, the number of churches within its special influence will be greatly increased, and the call for its supplies will be greatly multiplied. Already we have assurances of the confidence of many among our brethren of the Old School Presbyterian Church, and of their readiness to unite with us in making LANE a fountain of blessing to both ourselves and them, and to the kingdom of Christ in our land and in the world.

ANNUAL REPORT OF THE TREASURER

OF THE

BOARD OF TRUSTEES OF LANE THEOLOGICAL SEMINARY,

MAY 13, 1868.

RECEIPTS.			
Balance on hand May 9, 1867.		$3,011 17	
Ground Rents.........................	$8,038 55		
Interest.................................	3,681 19		
Donations..............................	235 00		
Bills Receivable.....................	5,517 42		
Educational Fund...................	100 00		
Van Vleck Library Fund..........	876 10		
Van Vleck Library Fund Investments.................................	2,778 13		
Professor D. H. Allen...............	900 00		
D. T. Woodbury Estate.............	3,525 00		
Boarding-house Building..........	916 00		
Yandes Scholarships................	166 26		
Sawyer Scholarships...............	188 14		
Ward and Condit Scholarships...	120 00	27,041 79	$30,052 96
DISBURSEMENTS.			
Salaries..............................	8 208 34		
Expense Account....................	3,215 31		
Interest...............................	214 16		
Educational Fund...................	105 00		
Endowment Fund....................	2,829 90		
Endowment Fund Investments..	6,066 88		
Van Vleck Library Fund..........	766 00		
Van Vleck Library Fund Investments.................................	4,000 00		
Yandes Scholarships................	165 00		
Sawyer Scholarships...............	280 00		
Ward and Condit Scholarships...	440 00	26,290 59	
Balance on hand in deposit Fourth Nat. Bank, Cin.....		3,762 37	$30,052 96
This balance belongs to the following accounts:			
Educational Fund..............	134 80		
Van Vleck Library Fund....	120 08		
Professor D. H. Allen.........	900 00		
Woodbury Legacy.............	236 25		
Boarding-house Building....	916 00		
Yandes Scholarships..........	221 63		
Sawyer Scholarships..........	192 74		
Ward & Condit Scholarships	363 50		
Endowment Fund..............	677 37	$3,762 37	

INVESTED FUNDS.

The amount of INVESTED FUNDS belonging to the Seminary is $46,600, of which $35,500 belong to the Endowment Fund, $7,100, to the Scholarship Fund; $4,000 to Van Vleck Library Fund.

THE ENDOWMENT FUND INVESTMENTS, by collection of notes, and first payment of Woodbury Legacy, have been increased during the past year $6,500, and consist at present of $25,500 United States Government 6 per cent. bonds, payable in gold, which the last year has yielded 8¾ per cent.; and $10,000 Railroad bonds, which have yielded 6.65 per cent., exclusive of government tax.

In addition to the $35,500 thus invested, there is in BILLS RECEIVABLE belonging to the Endowment Fund, $6,542 32, $4,000 of which is secured by mortgage on real estate, and paying interest at 8 per cent. per annum; $1,200 subscription to the Endowment Fund, and paying interest at 6 per cent.; also $1,342 32 in notes against different parties, given a long time since as donations to the Seminary, nearly all of which are past due, and probably will never be paid.

Besides this belonging to the Endowment Fund, there is $3,000 New Castle & Richmond Railroad bonds, with interest coupons 7 per cent. unpaid since February 25, 1860. By a mutual agreement with other bondholders, this claim, several years ago, was placed in the hands of R. B. Pullen, Esq., who assumed the collection of the same for 16¾ per cent., he paying all costs and attorneys' fees. The attorneys report favorably upon the claim, and expect soon to realize the whole amount. $300, notes against Reading Cemetery Association, dated June 1, 1859, are in the hands of William Cornell, Esq.. for collection; who reports that he will probably be able to collect at least part of the amount.

Also, deed of 160 acres of land in Dallas County, Missouri—in which the Western Female Seminary, at Oxford, has an equal interest. In order to have the same properly entered on the books, and appear among other assets of the Seminary, the half interest has been valued at $100.

From the foregoing statement it will be observed that the whole amount belonging to the Endowment Fund is $45,442 32; $40,500 of which are paying investments, and have yielded the past year an average of nearly 8 per cent. on this amount.

GROUND RENTS.

The other and most important source of revenue to the Seminary is GROUND RENTS, which, including rent of lot on Walnut street, Cincinnati, have yielded the past year $8,038 55, which is $1,730 40 in excess of amount collected the year previous. This increase is to be accounted for by the fact, that lots leased during the past year have increased the revenue at least $1,000, and many have paid who have been for a long while in arrears. Lots leased the past year will furnish a still further increase the next year. The annual rent of all lots now leased, as shown by Mr. T. M. Hinkle's report, is $9,594 29, and the amount outstanding as shown by the collector's books is $2,488 64, the most of which has only been due since 21st of April, and will probably be paid within the next sixty days.

LIBRARY FUND.

The VAN VLECK LIBRARY FUND by the collection of amount left in Europe by Professor Day, and the accumulation of interest, has, during the past year, increased its investments from $2,500 to $4,000, which amount, by direction of the Executive Committee, has been invested in stock of the Fourth National Bank of Cincinnati, which during the past year has declared dividends amounting to 10 per cent.

SCHOLARSHIP FUNDS.

Two YANDES SCHOLARSHIPS have in invested funds $2,500 Indianapolis, Pittsburg & Cleveland Railroad bonds, interest 7 per cent., payable in New York, which, after deducting government tax, has yielded what is equivalent to 6.65 per cent.

Two WARD AND CONDIT SCHOLARSHIPS have in invested funds $2,000 Cincinnati, Richmond & Chicago Railroad bonds payable as above, and exclusive of government tax have yielded the same rate of interest.

Two Sawyer Scholarships have in invested funds $2,600 of Bellefontaine Railroad stock, which the last year have declared dividends amounting to $6\frac{1}{2}$ per cent.

The whole amount received on Scholarship Funds during the year, as interest and dividend, has been $474 40, and the amount drawn against the same has been $885, showing that the amount drawn in excess of current receipts has been $410 60.

BEQUEST.

Since the last Annual Meeting of the Board, Mr. D. T. Woodbury, of Columbus, Ohio, a former member of Professor Morris' church, has died, leaving a legacy to the Seminary of $15,000: $10,000 of which is for the Endowment Fund; $4,000 for the Scholarship Fund; and $1,000 for the Library Fund. The first payment on this legacy; $2,750 (less government tax 6 per cent. $225), has already been received, and the amount invested in United States Government bonds. The other payments will probably be made in six, twelve, and eighteen months, or within two years.

The insurance on Boarding-house Building (which a few weeks since was so much injured by fire as in the judgment of the Executive Committee to make it unwise to repair) has been collected, and the amount, $916, passed to the credit of a new building. The estimated cost of the New Boarding-house Building is $18,000, to be completed if possible by the opening of the next term. The Seminary to pay $10,000 for the new building, and whatever it cost in excess of this amount has been generously donated by one of the trustees, and $2,000 has also been subscribed by another member of the board, which, with the $916 insurance already collected, leaves $7,084 to be provided for.

The present insurance on buildings and library, is as follows: $10,000 on Seminary building; $10,000 on Library building; $3,000 on Chapel building; $3,000 on Nelson house; $3,000 on Morris house; and $6,000 on the Library. Making in all $35,000.

From the report thus made it will be seen, that the sources of income for paying salaries, and other expenses of the Seminary, which are GROUND RENTS on INTEREST and DONATIONS, have yielded the past year $11,740 58.   And the expenses aside from assessment for opening Chapel street have been $11,423 65, showing that the receipts the past year have exceeded current expenses $316 93.   It is to be remembered, however, that the two newly elected professors have but recently entered upon their duties, and that the advance of salaries to the other professors did not take effect until the 1st of November and December.   The amount needed, therefore, to pay salaries the next year, without any increase in the number of professors, will be about $3,500 more than has been paid the last year. The current expenses of the next year can not be safely estimated at less than $15,000, and the receipts belonging to the Endowment Fund (including increase of ground rents), will not be likely to exceed $13,000, showing a probable deficiency of $2,000, which it is to be hoped will be provided for at the present meeting of the board. All of which is respectfully submitted.

F. V. CHAMBERLAIN, TREASURER.

The Committee to whom the above was referred have examined the items, with the vouchers therefor, and find it correct.

Walnut Hills, May 14, 1868.   PRESERVED SMITH,

JAMES TAYLOR,

COMMITTEE.